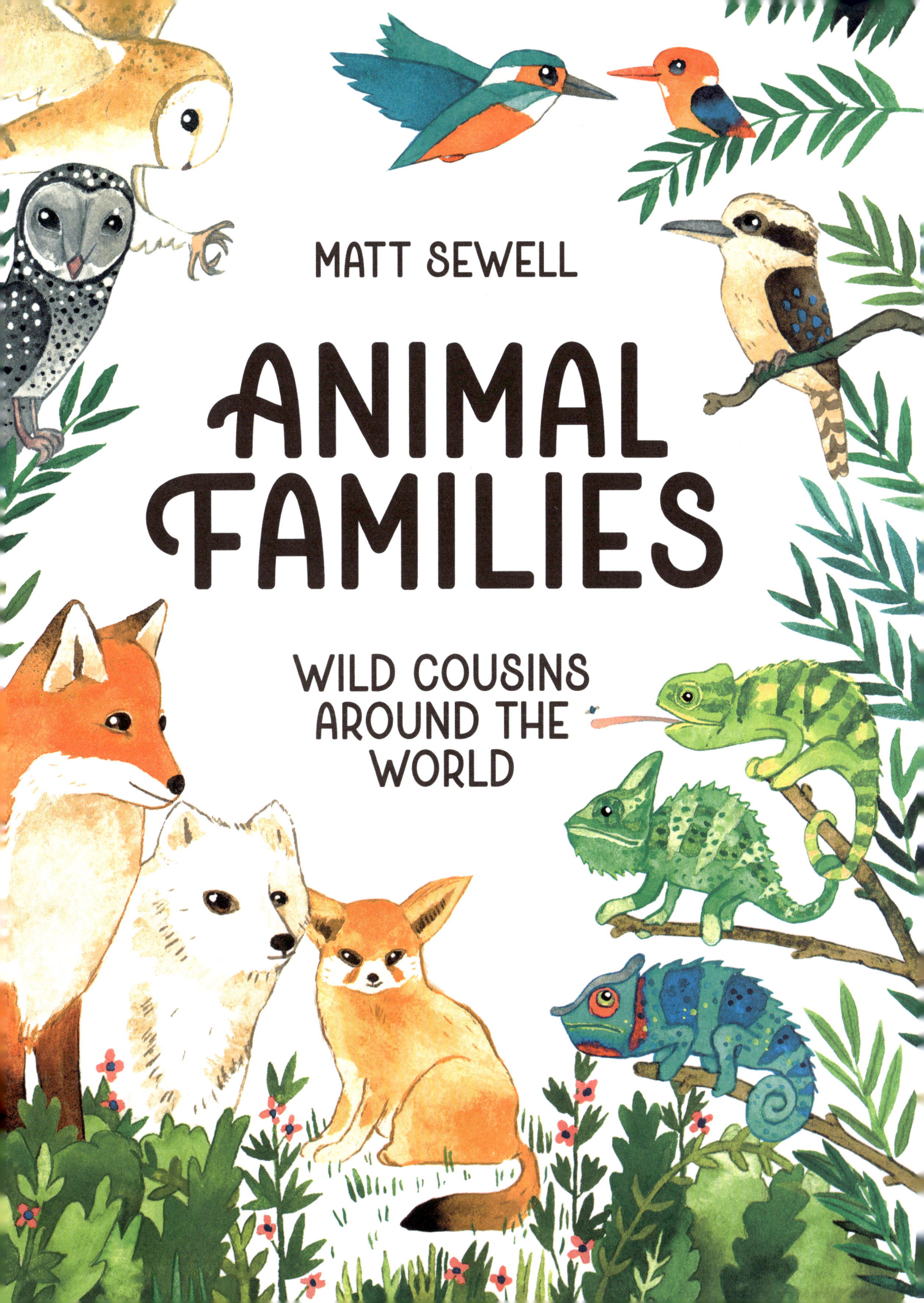

For my goldfinches, Romy & Mae

HODDER CHILDREN'S BOOKS
First published in Great Britain in 2025 by
Hodder and Stoughton

Text and illustrations copyright © Matt Sewell 2025

Matt Sewell has asserted his right under the Copyright, Designs
and Patents Act 1988 to be identified as the author of this work.

All rights reserved. A CIP catalogue record for this book
is available from the British Library.

Natural history consultant: Dr Ross Piper

HB ISBN: 978-1-444-97706-6
E-book ISBN: 978-1-444-97707-3

1 3 5 7 9 10 8 6 4 2

Printed in Dubai

Hodder Children's Books
An imprint of
Hachette Children's Group
Part of Hodder and Stoughton
Carmelite House, 50 Victoria Embankment
London EC4Y 0DZ

An Hachette UK Company
www.hachette.co.uk
www.hachettechildrens.co.uk

The authorised representative in the EEA is
Hachette Ireland, 8 Castlecourt Centre,
Castleknock Road, Castleknock,
Dublin 15, D15 YF6A, Ireland

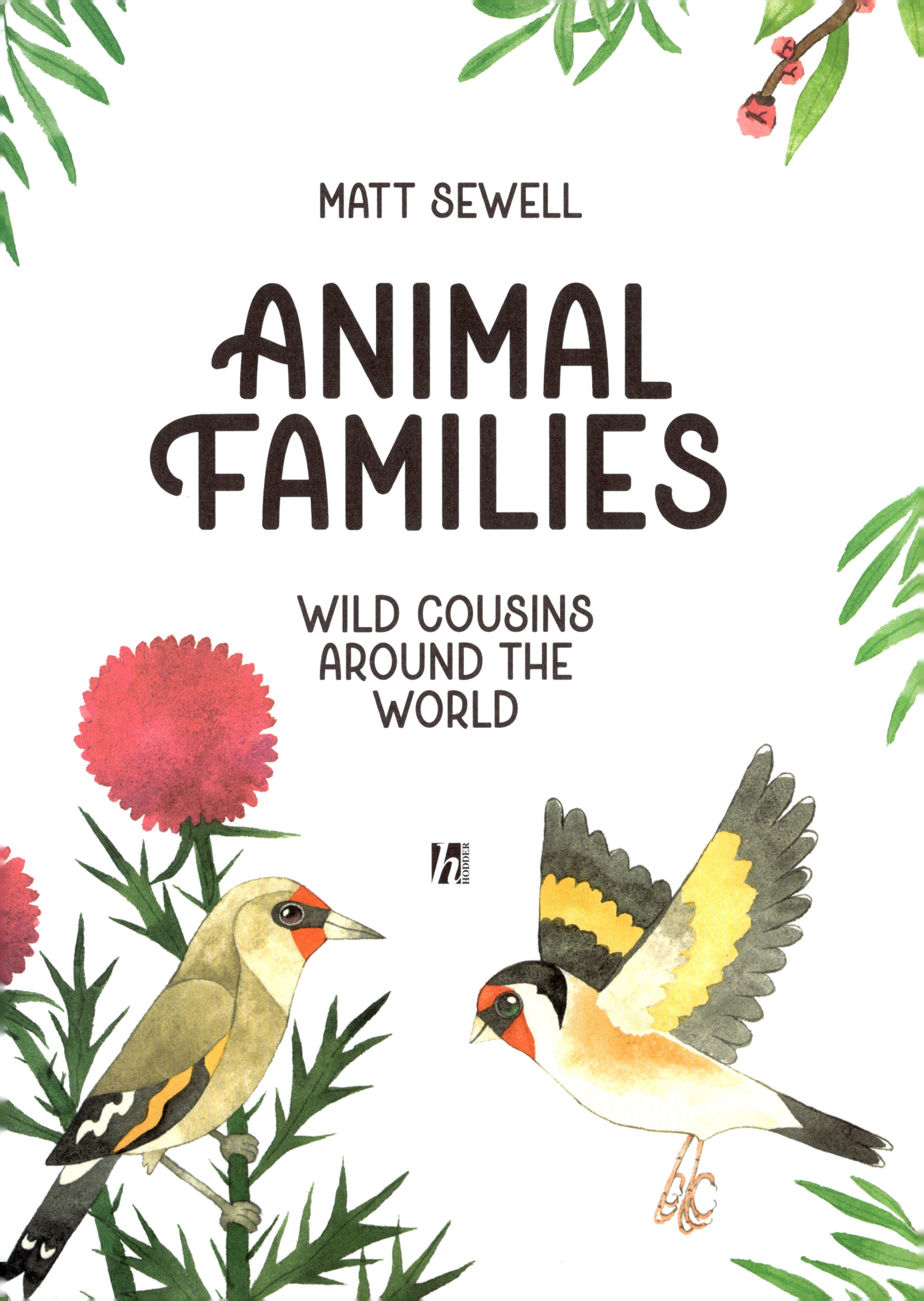

CONTENTS

5	Meet the Families!
6–7	Dolphins
8–9	Foxes
10–11	Squirrels
12–13	The sun bear versus the polar bear
14–15	Moles
16–17	Raccoons and other family members
18–19	The European badger versus the honey badger
20–21	Goldfinches
22–23	Kingfishers
24–25	The European robin versus the Japanese robin
26–27	Falcons
28–29	Barn owls
30–31	Magpies
32–33	The Goliath birdeater versus the peacock tarantula
34–35	Tiger beetles
36–37	Swallowtails
38–39	Hawkmoths
40–41	Jumping spiders
42–43	Cobras
44–45	Chameleons
46–47	The ocellate river stingray versus the bluespotted ribbontail ray
48	Glossary

MEET THE FAMILIES!

So far, scientists have identified and named around 1.2 MILLION different plant and animal species on our planet. That's a whole lot of life! And lots and lots of animal families . . .

Species, or types of animals, are organised into FAMILY groups based on the things they have in common. Take the **URSIDAE** family (that's bears, to you and me). There are eight members in this furry family, and in turn, they all belong to an ORDER, or a bigger group, called **CARNIVORA**. Carnivora is made up of 12 different animal families that includes the cat family and the dog family. In turn, orders belong to an even larger group called a CLASS, and the Carnivora belong in a class called **MAMMALIA**, which includes all mammals.

Putting animals and plants into different groups helps us to understand the difference between one living thing and another, and how they might be related.

In this book we are going to look at some fascinating animal FAMILIES. Some animals may live continents apart and appear to lead very different lives – but take a closer look at the shape of a beak or the curve of a claw and you will see that they might be related. And of course, not all cousins look alike. The laughing kookaburra of Australia may not wear the brightly coloured feathers of the common kingfisher of Europe, but they are family all the same.

You could say the same about us humans – we are spread all over the world, and our lives can seem very different, but WE are all family too!

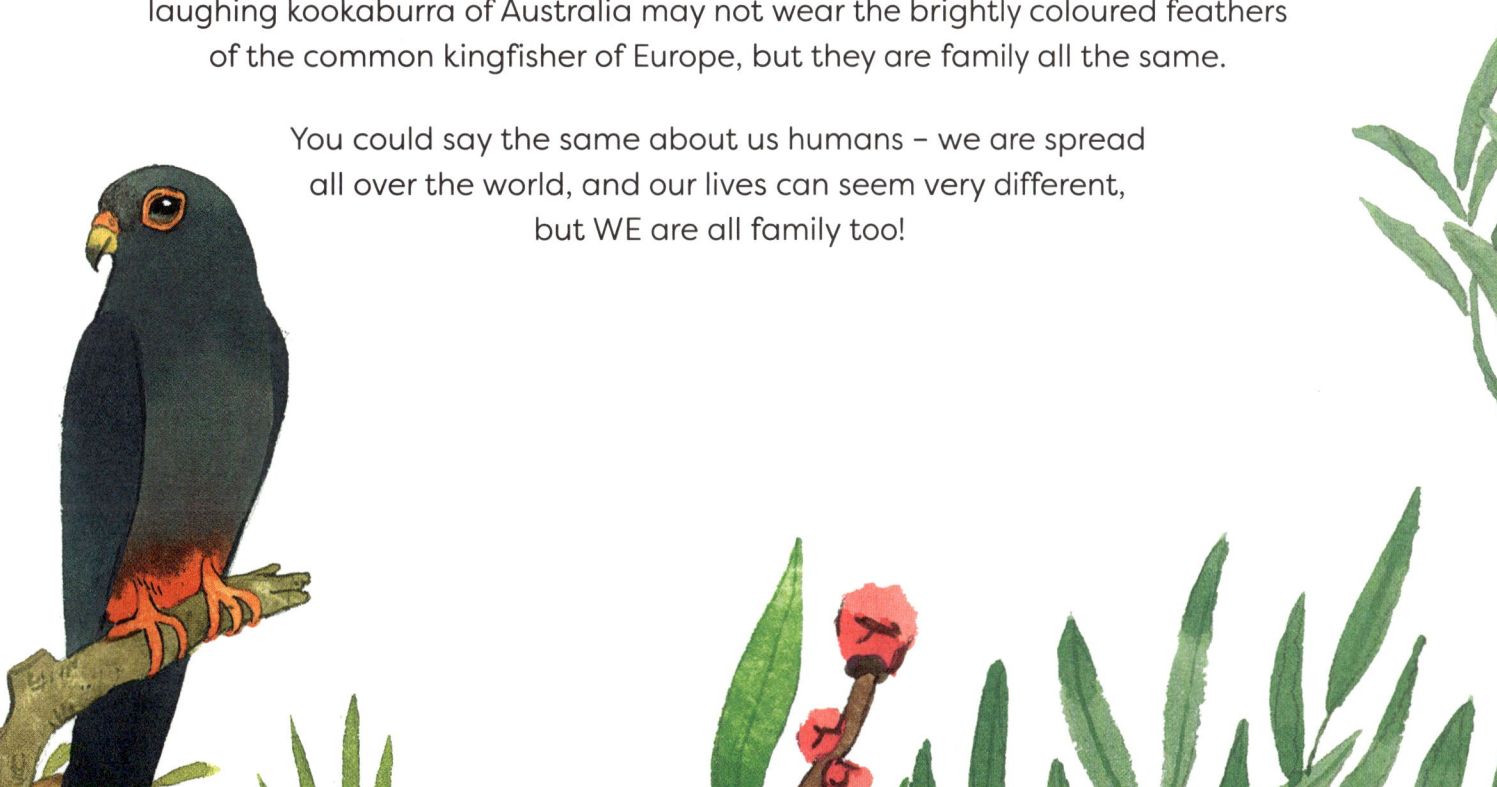

DOLPHINS

Sociable dolphins hang out in groups called **PODS** in oceans around the world. Dolphins are mammals, not fish, so they need to come to the surface of the water to breathe. However, when underwater they can hold their breath for an amazing seven minutes!

ORDER: Artiodactyla
FAMILY: Delphinidae (oceanic dolphins)
Oceanic dolphins form the biggest dolphin family, with 38 members.

COMMON BOTTLENOSE DOLPHIN
Temperate and tropical waters around the world

BRAIN-BOXES

Dolphins communicate using clicks and whistles and they have different whistles for each member of their pod, a bit like names. They are also able to sleep with one side of their brain awake so that they can stay alert to danger at all times.

HECTOR'S DOLPHIN
New Zealand

DUSKY DOLPHIN

All dolphins are excellent swimmers and love to leap and spin out of the water, but high-energy **DUSKY DOLPHINS** are the true gymnasts. They have even been spotted performing synchronised swimming routines!

DUSKY DOLPHIN
New Zealand, South America, southwestern Africa

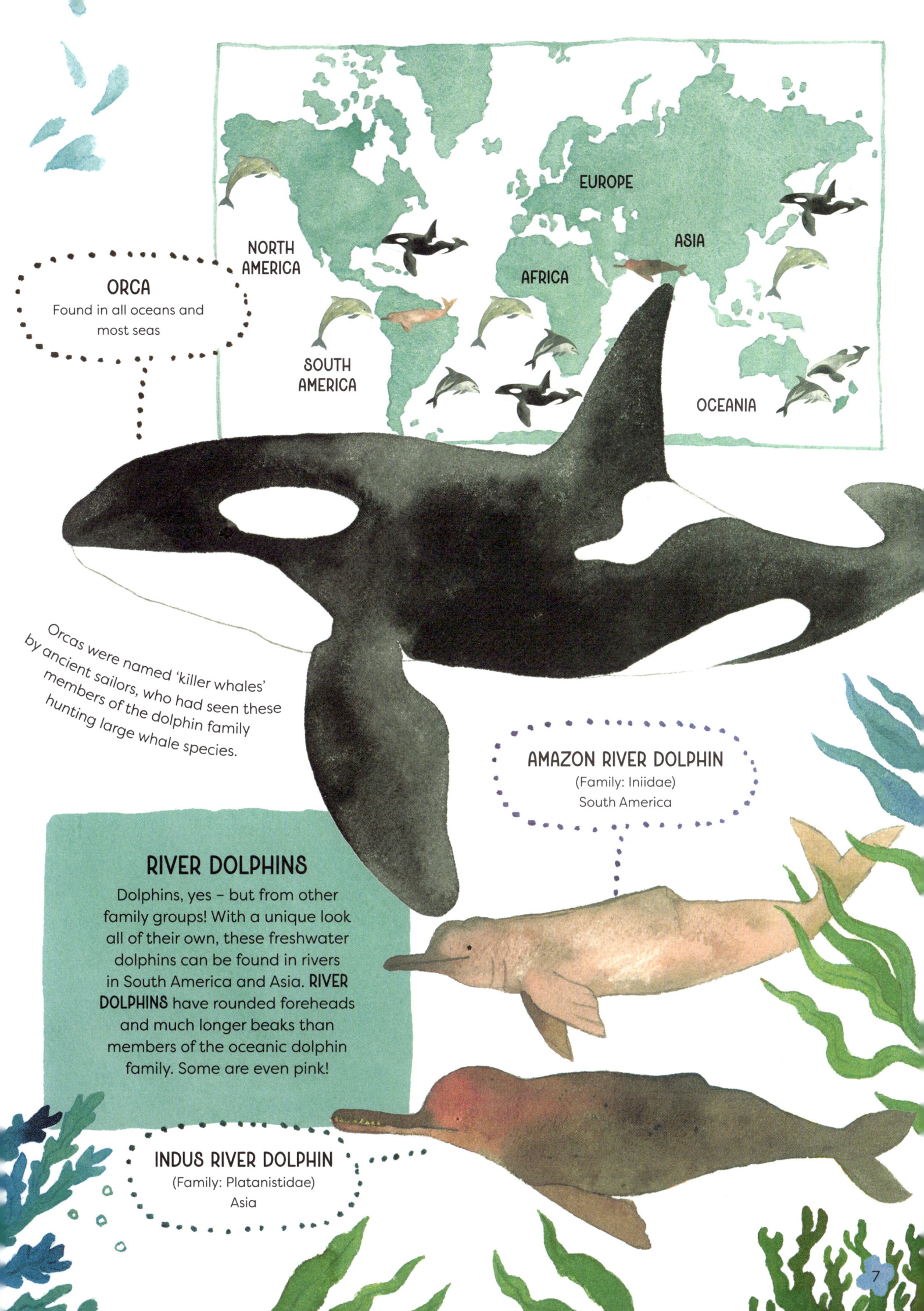

ORCA
Found in all oceans and most seas

Orcas were named 'killer whales' by ancient sailors, who had seen these members of the dolphin family hunting large whale species.

AMAZON RIVER DOLPHIN
(Family: Iniidae)
South America

RIVER DOLPHINS

Dolphins, yes – but from other family groups! With a unique look all of their own, these freshwater dolphins can be found in rivers in South America and Asia. **RIVER DOLPHINS** have rounded foreheads and much longer beaks than members of the oceanic dolphin family. Some are even pink!

INDUS RIVER DOLPHIN
(Family: Platanistidae)
Asia

ORDER: Carnivora
FAMILY: Canidae
As well as foxes, this family includes wolves, coyotes, jackals and . . . your pet dog!

FOXES

Foxes live on almost every continent in the world and have adapted well to many different habitats. Night-time **EXPLORERS**, these omnivorous mammals get a bad press in fairy stories. They are often portrayed as sly and cunning, but they are in fact savvy animals to be admired.

DESERT LIVING

The smallest member of the family also has the biggest ears! The **FENNEC FOX** is perfectly built for desert life. It keeps cool by losing heat through its large ears and has extremely furry paws to protect them from the hot sand that it scampers over.

CAPE FOX
South Africa

FENNEC FOX
North Africa

FOX TALK

If you live in a town or a city, you might be familiar with the 'wow-wow-wow' call of the fox – or the horrible screeches it makes when it is fighting. Foxes are chatty animals, and have different calls for communicating with their young, greeting other foxes or expressing alarm.

RED FOX
North America, Europe, Asia, North Africa, Australia

NORTH AMERICA
SOUTH AMERICA
EUROPE
AFRICA
ASIA
OCEANIA

BENGAL FOX
India, Pakistan

TIBETAN FOX
Tibet, China, India

ARCTIC FOX
Arctic regions of the Northern Hemisphere

The Bengal fox has a very long, extremely fluffy black-tipped tail.

COSTUME CHANGE

In winter, the beautiful white coat of the **ARCTIC FOX** gets thicker to protect it from chilly temperatures. In summer, it sheds this luxurious outfit for a thinner, darker coat, which helps it to blend in with its habitat once the snow has melted.

SQUIRRELS

Whether leaping and gliding between trees or scurrying through underground burrows, these **CUTE** rodents with fluffy tails have a strong family resemblance. Like most families though, they do have their quirks . . .

ORDER: Rodentia
FAMILY: Sciuridae
The squirrel family includes tree squirrels, ground squirrels and flying squirrels.

SOUTHERN FLYING SQUIRREL
North America

SQUIRRELS MIGHT FLY
The **SOUTHERN FLYING SQUIRREL** should really be called the southern gliding squirrel. They have a fold of skin between their front and back limbs called a patagium. When they spread their limbs out in an 'X' shape, the skin acts like a parachute.

NATURE'S LITTLE HELPERS
As winter approaches, squirrels bury nuts and seeds, ready for when food becomes scarce. Sometimes they forget to retrieve their buried treasures, so some seeds will sprout and grow into baby trees the following spring.

EURASIAN RED SQUIRREL
Europe, Asia

PREVOST'S SQUIRREL
Southeast Asia

MALABAR GIANT SQUIRREL
India

PICNIC THIEVES
They may look cute and have the ability to charm us for picnic scraps, but since their introduction into Europe in the 1800s, **GREY SQUIRRELS** have been bad news for red squirrels. Sturdier than their red-haired cousins, greys drive the reds out of their favourite habitats.

HARRIS' ANTELOPE SQUIRREL
North America: Arizona, New Mexico; Mexico.

The desert-dwelling Harris' antelope squirrel holds its fluffy tail over its back as protection against the sun.

GREY SQUIRREL
Europe, North America

THE SUN BEAR . . .

Bears belong to the **URSIDAE** family, and they all have furry bodies and short bushy tails – but they don't all look alike or behave the same. Many of their differences depend on where they live. These two may look cuddly, but don't forget they are wild animals with big, impressive claws!

The **SUN BEAR** of Southeast Asia spends most of its day lolling in the trees. Named for the golden patch of fur on its chest, the sun bear has a short, sleek coat to help it cope with the tropical heat. Its long, curved claws help it to climb trees, to strip bark to get to tasty insects hiding underneath, or to tear apart beehives, ant nests and termite mounds. They also eat fruit.

Male sun bears grow up to 1.2 m in length

Thick skin under fur protects the bear from angry bees

SLURP!
The SUN BEAR is the smallest member of the family, but it has an impressively long tongue. At around 25 centimetres (cm) long, it is the perfect tool for reaching inside insect nests.

Hairless pads on paws

WHEN IS A BEAR NOT A BEAR?
When it is a koala bear! Once thought to be a bear by early European settlers in Australia, a koala is in fact a marsupial. It is also the only living member of its family (Phascolarctidae). But don't worry, it has other koalas to hang out with.

VERSUS THE POLAR BEAR

The **POLAR BEAR** lives in and around the waters of the frozen Arctic. Its large, webbed paws act like paddles when it is swimming and are perfect snowshoes for prowling around on slippery ice. A layer of blubbery fat under the polar bear's thick waterproof coat keeps it warm in its cold, watery habitat. And under all that fur, its skin is actually black! This also helps keep the bear warm, as dark colours absorb the heat of the sun better.

Narrow head with long muzzle

Male polar bears can grow up to 2.5 m in length

Short, unretractable claws

I SMELL LUNCH

One of the largest bears in the family, the polar bear is a skilled hunter. It also has an amazing sense of smell and can sniff out a seal's breathing hole in the ice from more than a kilometre away!

BROLAR BEARS

The polar bear is closely related to the brown bear. In Canada, Russia and Alaska, USA, the two types of bears have been known to mate, producing a hybrid bear we could call a 'brolar bear'!

MOLES

With homes in North America, Asia and Europe, these small, velvety-furred mammals cannot see very well but they have incredibly sensitive snouts. Most species of mole are underground burrowing animals, but some, such as desmans, prefer to hang out in the water.

ORDER: Eulipotyphla
FAMILY: Talpidae
This little family also includes shrew moles and desmans.

AMERICAN SHREW MOLE
North America

At less than 5 cm long, this is the tiniest mole in the family.

STAR OF THE SHOW
The hamster-sized **STAR-NOSED MOLE** has a snout quite unlike any other! Made of 22 fleshy tentacles, this impressive nose helps it to feel around for food in the dark underground tunnels that it digs.

STAR-NOSED MOLE
North America

PYRENEAN DESMAN
Spain, Portugal, French Pyrenees

This semi-aquatic mole is an excellent swimmer, with a nose like a snorkel.

NORTH AMERICA
EUROPE
ASIA
AFRICA
SOUTH AMERICA
OCEANIA

JAPANESE SHREW MOLE
Japan

TUNNEL VISION
Around two-thirds of mole species spend most of their time underground in a network of tunnels that they add to throughout their lives. With their paddlelike feet, sharp claws and short, strong forelimbs, a **EUROPEAN MOLE** can dig up to 200 m of tunnel every day.

EUROPEAN MOLE
Europe and westernmost Asia

HAIRY-TAILED MOLE
North America

15

ORDER: Carnivora
FAMILY: Procyonidae
The Procyonidae family includes raccoons, ringtails, cacomistles, coatis, kinkajous, olingos and olinguitos.

RACCOONS
and other family members

Skilled climbers, expert problem-solvers and unfussy eaters, raccoons can be found far and wide across the **AMERICAS**. They live in forests, on farmland, near water and even – to the annoyance of some human residents – in towns and cities.

KINKAJOU
Mexico, Central and South America

The cousin with a sweet tooth, the kinkajou raids beehives for its sugar fix.

PYGMY RACCOON
Cozumel island, Mexico

TRASH PANDA
The **COMMON RACCOON** can be found in the town and in the countryside. This clever creature has adapted well to city life and rummages through rubbish bins for food. This behaviour has earned it the nickname 'trash panda'. Raccoons have very nimble fingers and have even been seen opening fridge doors.

COMMON RACCOON
North America

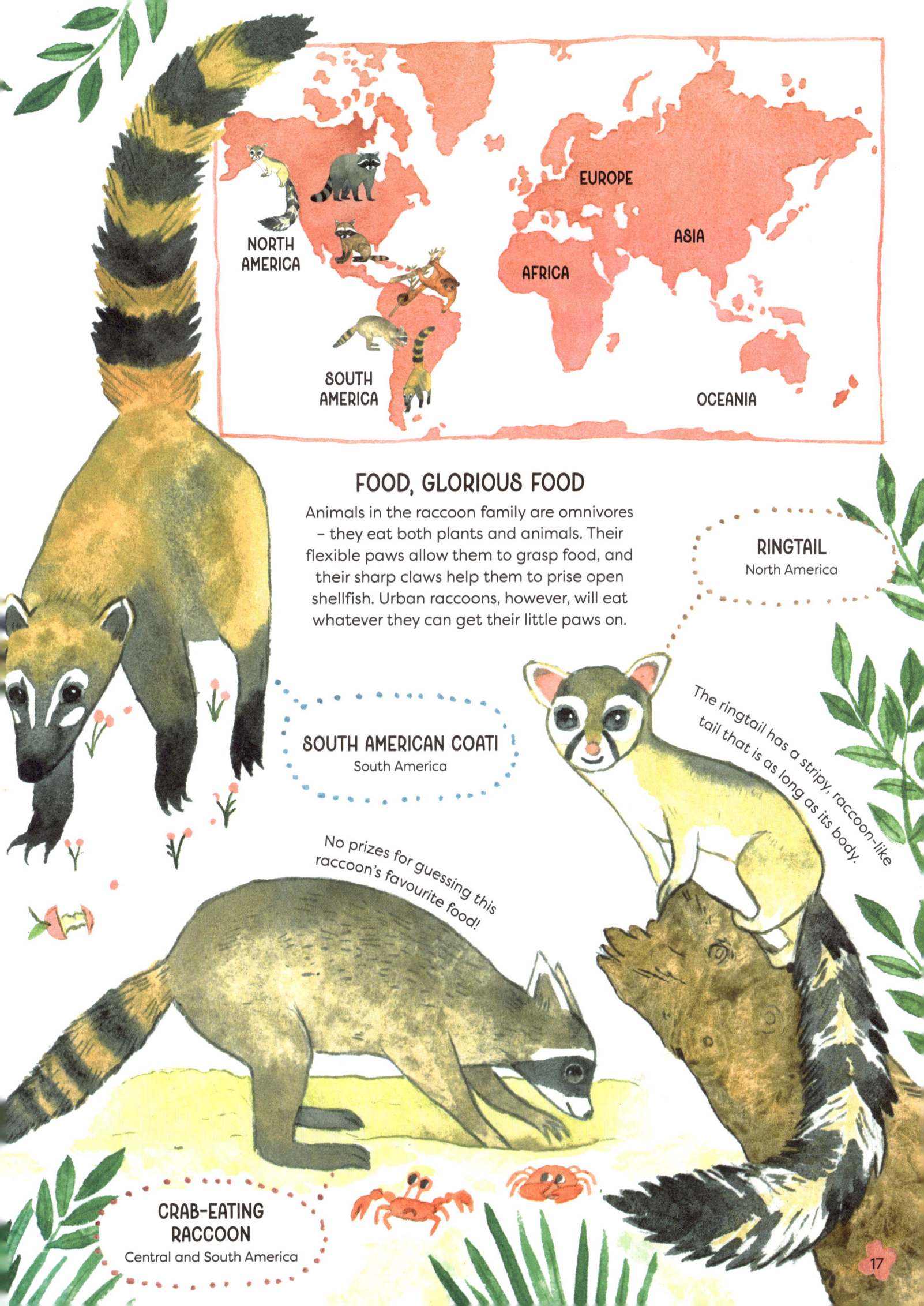

FOOD, GLORIOUS FOOD

Animals in the raccoon family are omnivores – they eat both plants and animals. Their flexible paws allow them to grasp food, and their sharp claws help them to prise open shellfish. Urban raccoons, however, will eat whatever they can get their little paws on.

RINGTAIL
North America

The ringtail has a stripy, raccoon-like tail that is as long as its body.

SOUTH AMERICAN COATI
South America

No prizes for guessing this raccoon's favourite food!

CRAB-EATING RACCOON
Central and South America

THE EUROPEAN BADGER...

Famously grumpy, stocky and with a distinctive trundling walk, badgers belong to the Mustelidae family, scattered across the globe in many different habitats. Some of this furry family look and behave very similarly. Others – such as the **HONEY BADGER** and the **EUROPEAN BADGER** – are more like very distant cousins who have never met!

This is the badger of classic European storybooks, with its sweet black-and-white striped face. The **EUROPEAN BADGER** is a sociable creature and, like many other species of badger, lives in close family groups. It can be found in Europe and western and central Asia.

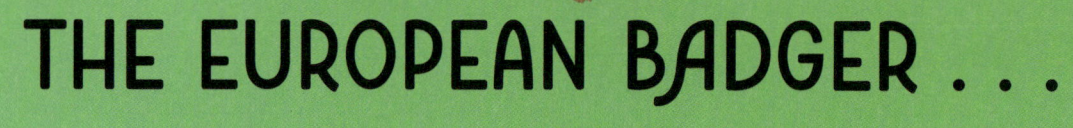

Large, wedge-shaped body

Fluffy ears that stick out from its head

Broad head with long muzzle

Powerful, stocky legs

Sharp claws, used for digging

HOME SWEET HOME

The **EUROPEAN BADGER** lives in underground burrows called setts. They are also very houseproud, keeping 'outdoor loos' and frequently lining their 'bedrooms' with fresh leaves!

VERSUS THE HONEY BADGER

Unlike the European badger, the **HONEY BADGER** is a loner. It will only mix with other honey badgers when it is time to start a family. The honey badger is more closely related to the weasel than to the European badger, which explains its little weasel-like face. The honey badger lives in Africa, Southwest Asia and on the Indian subcontinent.

TOUGH COOKIE

The honey badger is one tough little critter. It doesn't go looking for a fight, but when threatened, it will face up to its attacker. They have been known to get into scuffles with lions, hyenas and even pythons! Now that's brave.

Tiny ears on the side of its head

Thick grey stripe from the top of its head to the base of its tail

Small, flattened head with short muzzle

Long claws on front feet, perfect for digging – and fighting

Under the fur, skin is tough and loose

HOUSE THIEF!

The **HONEY BADGER** digs burrows to sleep in – but it is less fussy than its European relative. They will also sleep in old termite mounds, in holes under tree roots or in crevices between rocks. It will even take over burrows made by other animals, chasing off the original owner!

WHEN IS A BADGER NOT A BADGER?

When it is a Sunda stink badger! This little oddball found snuffling around forests in Indonesia and Malaysia is actually a relative of the skunk family (Mephitidae). Like a skunk, it can spray smelly chemicals from its bum when threatened.

ORDER: Passeriformes
FAMILY: Fringillidae
This bird family also includes chaffinches, bullfinches and rosefinches.

GOLDFINCHES

Mostly found in Europe and North America, these sociable **SONGBIRDS** belong to a large family also known as true finches. A group of goldfinches is called a 'charm', and with their brightly coloured feathers and sweet singing voices, it is easy to see why.

AMERICAN GOLDFINCH
North America

A RAY OF SUNSHINE

The show-off of the family, male **AMERICAN GOLDFINCHES** grow extra-bright yellow feathers during the mating season in order to attract maximum romantic attention.

LESSER GOLDFINCH
North and South America

The lesser goldfinch would come last in a goldfinch talent contest, as it has a rather wheezy-sounding song.

HIMALAYAN GOLDFINCH
Asia

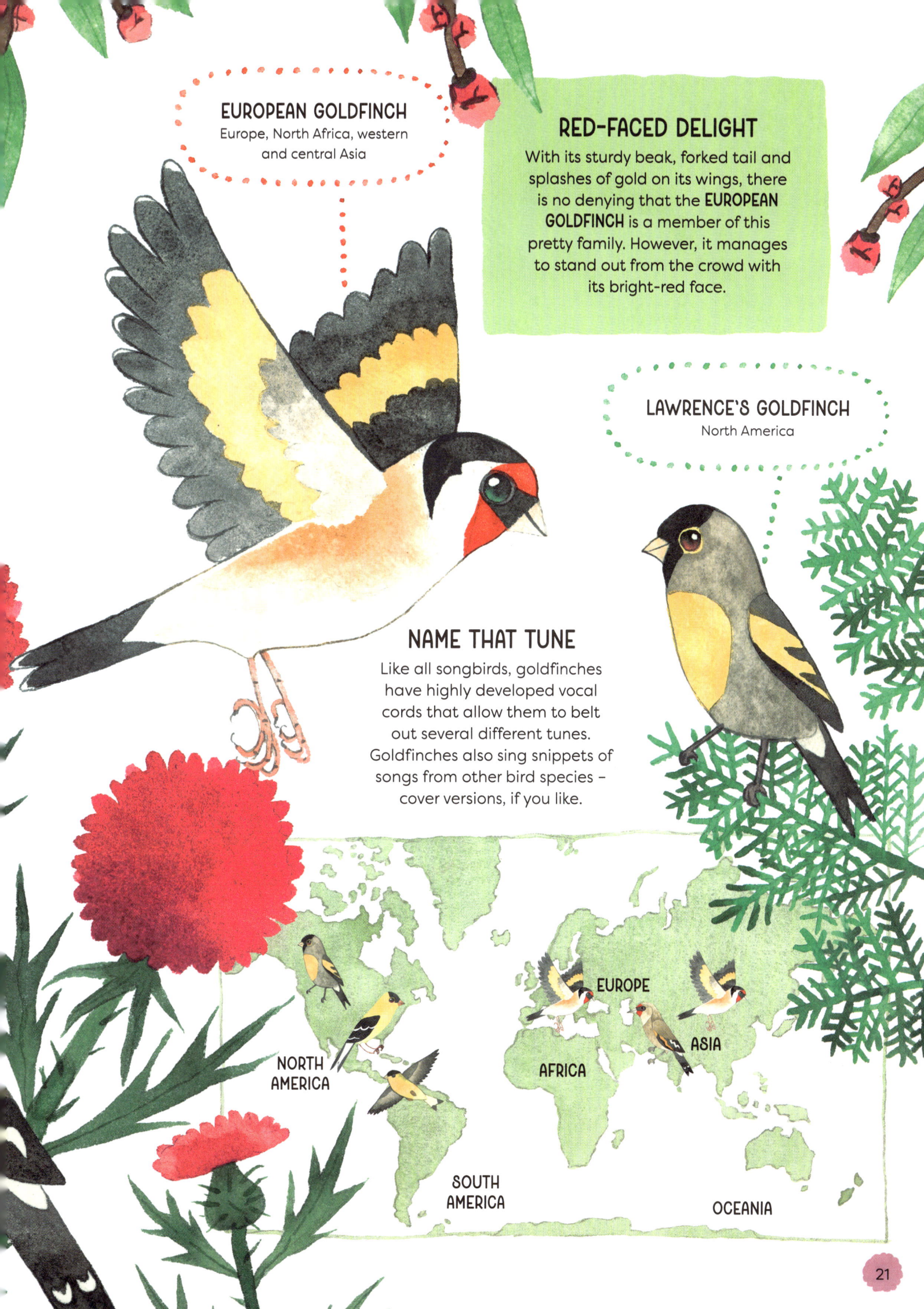

EUROPEAN GOLDFINCH
Europe, North Africa, western and central Asia

RED-FACED DELIGHT

With its sturdy beak, forked tail and splashes of gold on its wings, there is no denying that the **EUROPEAN GOLDFINCH** is a member of this pretty family. However, it manages to stand out from the crowd with its bright-red face.

LAWRENCE'S GOLDFINCH
North America

NAME THAT TUNE

Like all songbirds, goldfinches have highly developed vocal cords that allow them to belt out several different tunes. Goldfinches also sing snippets of songs from other bird species – cover versions, if you like.

NORTH AMERICA

SOUTH AMERICA

EUROPE

AFRICA

ASIA

OCEANIA

ORDER: Coraciiformes
FAMILY: Alcedinidae
This kingfisher family includes tree, river and water kingfishers.

KINGFISHERS

As their name suggests, these shy little birds with super-long beaks are **EXPERT FISHERS**. But blink and you might miss them, as they dart around rivers, waterways and woodlands at top speed. This feathery family can be found on every continent apart from Antarctica.

COMMON KINGFISHER
Europe, Asia, North Africa

FLASHES OF COLOUR
The **COMMON KINGFISHER** has spectacular feathers that shimmer a vibrant green or blue depending on the light. Listen out for a high-pitched 'peep!' as they flash past – they always call out as they fly.

WOODLAND KINGFISHER
Africa

The cutest family member, this kingfisher has a bright red beak that makes it look like a perfect, pocket-sized toy.

BLACK-BACKED DWARF KINGFISHER
Indian subcontinent, Southeast Asia

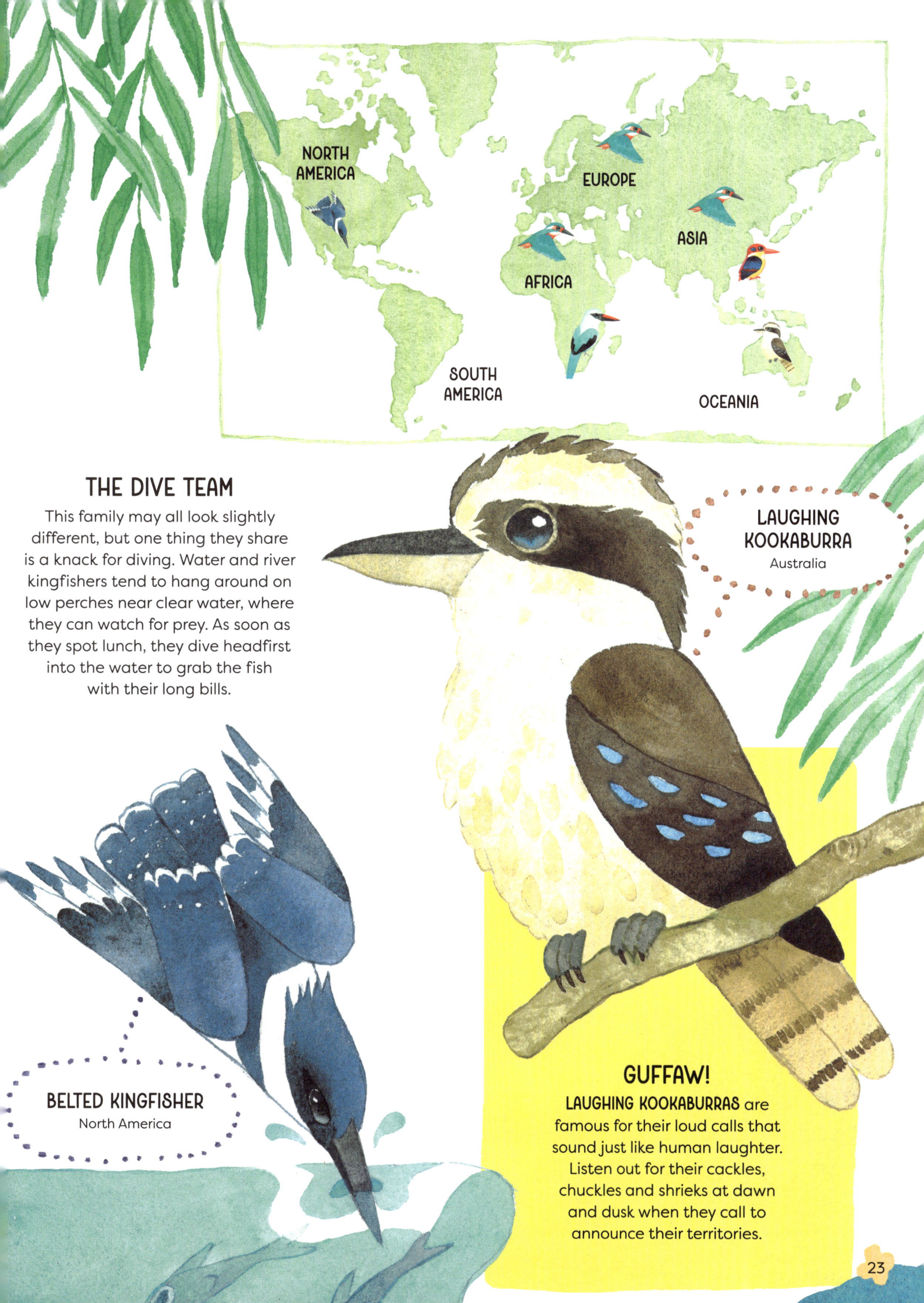

NORTH AMERICA
EUROPE
ASIA
AFRICA
SOUTH AMERICA
OCEANIA

THE DIVE TEAM
This family may all look slightly different, but one thing they share is a knack for diving. Water and river kingfishers tend to hang around on low perches near clear water, where they can watch for prey. As soon as they spot lunch, they dive headfirst into the water to grab the fish with their long bills.

LAUGHING KOOKABURRA
Australia

BELTED KINGFISHER
North America

GUFFAW!
LAUGHING KOOKABURRAS are famous for their loud calls that sound just like human laughter. Listen out for their cackles, chuckles and shrieks at dawn and dusk when they call to announce their territories.

THE EUROPEAN ROBIN...

Scattered across Europe, Asia and Africa, robins are best known for the feathery splashes of colour on their throats and chests. These two perky little **SONGBIRDS** may live on opposite sides of the world, but both belong to the Muscicapidae family.

Despite their name, orange-breasted **EUROPEAN ROBINS** can also be found in Siberia, Russia, and North Africa. These robins may look sweet, but they can be incredibly fierce. Face-offs between rivals usually start with a singing contest, and if that does not solve the dispute, they will fight – occasionally to the death!

Orange-red feathers stretching from throat to face

Small, plump body

Brown tail and wing feathers

JUICY WORMS

The European robin can often be seen hanging around people digging the soil in their gardens. They know that when the soil is turned over it will reveal fresh insects and worms for them to swoop down and devour.

WHEN IS A ROBIN NOT A ROBIN?

This pink robin found in Australia belongs to a different family – the Petroicidae – but it is a robin by name and is distinctly robin-ish, so let's not quibble! Unlike the European robin, this feathery beauty is very shy.

VERSUS THE JAPANESE ROBIN

A distant relation of the European robin, the **JAPANESE ROBIN** still has the family's sweet looks. These shy little robins live on the islands of Japan. They might be hard to spot, but listen out for their loud, pretty song. Female Japanese robins will sing while they are nest-building, as though happy in their work!

COUNTRYSIDE LIVING

The European robin is a common sight in towns and cities, but the Japanese robin prefers the simpler country life. They make their home in forests, and if you are lucky, you might spot them hopping around in the shady undergrowth of the forest floor.

Entire head is covered in bright red feathers

Orange tail feathers

Soft grey feathered body

WHAT'S IN A NAME?

All robins are insectivores, which means they dine mainly on insects. The scientific name for the Japanese robin is *Larvivora akahige*, which means 'larva eater'.

FALCONS

ORDER: Falconiformes
FAMILY: Falconidae
This skilled family of hunters includes birds with the name 'kestrel' and 'falcon'.

Falcons are the superheroes of the bird world, with amazing powers of speed, intelligence and super-vision! They are **BIRDS OF PREY**, which means they are predatory hunters. Surprisingly, falcons are closely related to parrots and songbirds.

PEREGRINE FALCON
Worldwide, apart from Antarctica

PEREGRINE FALCON
The **PEREGRINE FALCON** is the fastest bird on the planet. When it dives through the air to catch its prey, it can reach speeds of up to 300 kilometres per hour (kph) – that's much, much faster than a cheetah running on land!

COLLARED FALCONET
Asia

FOX KESTREL
Africa

FAR-FLUNG FAMILY
Falcons are a truly global family and live in almost every kind of habitat, including deserts, forests and grasslands. These hunters will live anywhere they can find food! Shared family features include sharp talons, hooked bills and super-strong feet.

HOBBY
Europe, Asia, Africa

COMMON KESTREL
Europe, Asia, Africa, North America

COMMON KESTREL
All falcons are masters of flight. But kestrels, including the **COMMON KESTREL**, are especially famous for their 'hovering' technique. They do this by flying into the wind and beating their wings at speed, which allows them to stay in the same spot whilst eyeballing their next meal on the ground.

These acrobatic fliers can catch a dragonfly in mid-air!

RED-FOOTED FALCON
Europe, Asia

NORTH AMERICA
SOUTH AMERICA
EUROPE
AFRICA
ASIA
OCEANIA

BARN OWLS

Light of body and soft of feather, barn owls are ghostly **CREATURES OF THE NIGHT**. As they are nocturnal, you are more likely to hear them than see them, but don't expect the classic 'twit-twoo' – barn owls have an eerie screech. This feathery family can be found on almost every continent on Earth.

ORDER: Strigiformes
FAMILY: Tytonidae
This bird family includes barn, masked and grass owls.

Masked owls have a deep, rasping screech.

GREATER SOOTY OWL
Australia

AUSTRALIAN MASKED OWL
Australia, Papua New Guinea

WORLDWIDE TRAVELLER

COMMON BARN OWLS can live in almost any habitat (not just in barns), and are found in cities, forests and farmland. Wherever there is a good supply of small, tasty mammals, there will be barn owls nearby.

COMMON BARN OWL
Worldwide, apart from Antarctica

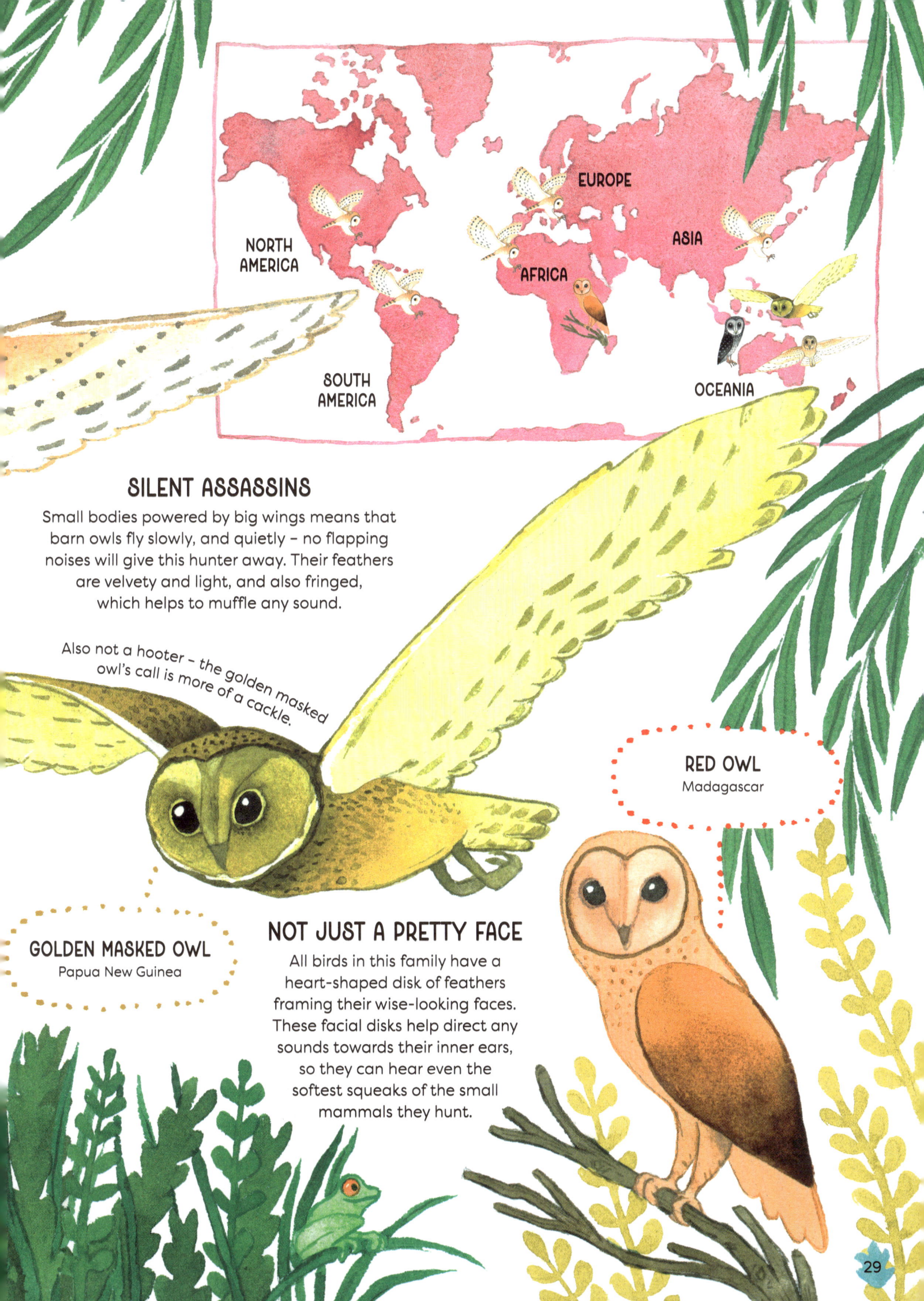

SILENT ASSASSINS

Small bodies powered by big wings means that barn owls fly slowly, and quietly – no flapping noises will give this hunter away. Their feathers are velvety and light, and also fringed, which helps to muffle any sound.

Also not a hooter – the golden masked owl's call is more of a cackle.

GOLDEN MASKED OWL
Papua New Guinea

RED OWL
Madagascar

NOT JUST A PRETTY FACE

All birds in this family have a heart-shaped disk of feathers framing their wise-looking faces. These facial disks help direct any sounds towards their inner ears, so they can hear even the softest squeaks of the small mammals they hunt.

MAGPIES

ORDER: Passeriformes
FAMILY: Corvidae
This big family also includes crows, ravens, rooks and jays.

A big character with a bold, strutting walk, the magpie can be found all over the world. They are intelligent birds with playful attitudes, so whoever decided that a group of magpies should be called a '**MISCHIEF OF MAGPIES**' summed these rowdy birds up perfectly.

EURASIAN MAGPIE
Europe

CLEVER CLOGS
The **EURASIAN MAGPIE** is one of the most intelligent birds in the world. Scientists have discovered that magpies are able to recognise themselves in a mirror and use tools. They have also been seen performing little funeral ceremonies when one of their flock dies.

YELLOW-BILLED MAGPIE
North America

RED-BILLED BLUE MAGPIE
Asia

CHATTERBOXES
Birds in this family may not have the sweetest voices, but some magpies can mimic noises made by other animals. In captivity, magpies have even mimicked human speech, repeating words and phrases such as 'Hi!' and 'I love you!'

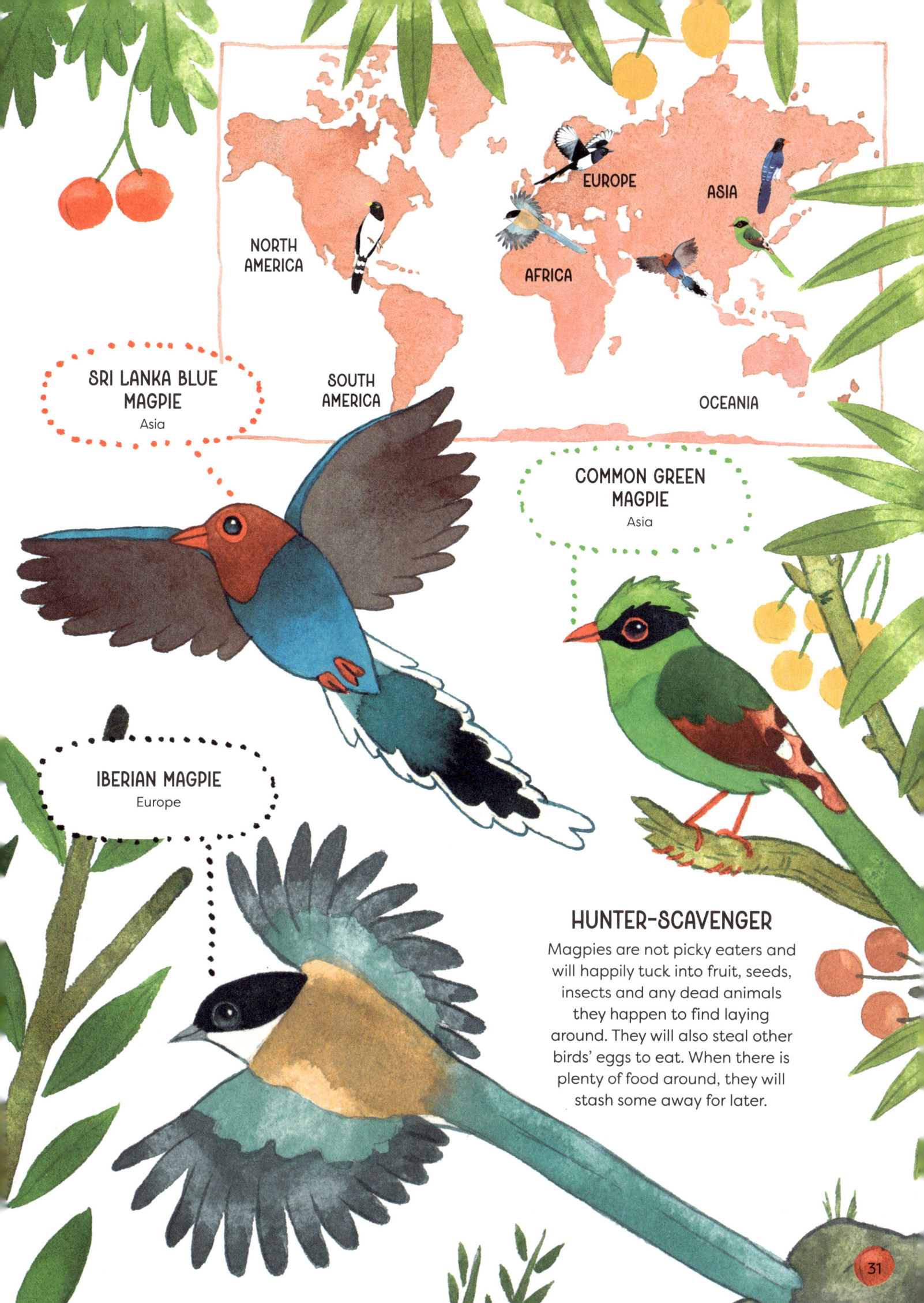

NORTH AMERICA

EUROPE

ASIA

AFRICA

SOUTH AMERICA

OCEANIA

SRI LANKA BLUE MAGPIE
Asia

COMMON GREEN MAGPIE
Asia

IBERIAN MAGPIE
Europe

HUNTER-SCAVENGER

Magpies are not picky eaters and will happily tuck into fruit, seeds, insects and any dead animals they happen to find laying around. They will also steal other birds' eggs to eat. When there is plenty of food around, they will stash some away for later.

THE GOLIATH BIRDEATER . . .

This fascinating duo belong to the tarantula family of spiders. There are more than 900 species of these venomous **ARACHNIDS**, and they all have hairy-looking bodies, eight eyes and – wait for it – fangs! Let's take a look at two with quite different lifestyles, living on two different continents.

Found in the rainforests of northern South America, the **GOLIATH BIRDEATER** can have a body of up to 10 cm long, with a leg span of around 30 cm! It is the largest spider on Earth by weight. It lives in deep burrows or beneath rocks and, being nocturnal, it emerges at night to roam the damp rainforest floor for its next meal.

Eight bristly legs

Pincer-like claws, with fangs folded up underneath

Two shorter 'legs' called pedipalps, used to grab prey

An assassin bug, the tarantula's dinner

BIRDEATER BY NAME

. . . but not by nature. Despite its name, this huge tarantula rarely eats birds. (Birds are tough to catch if you are a spider scuttling around on a forest floor.) **GOLIATH BIRDEATERS** feast mainly on large insects, other arachnids, worms – and the occasional rodent, lizard, snake or amphibian if they are especially hungry.

VERSUS THE PEACOCK TARANTULA

The amazing blue **PEACOCK TARANTULA** can be found in India. It is a forest-dwelling spider, so unlike its South American cousin who is a floor-scuttler, the peacock mostly hangs out high up in the trees, dining on passing flying insects. This pretty tarantula is half the size of the Goliath birdeater, with a 15-cm-long legspan.

Bright blue hairy body

Fangs used to inject venom into prey

Eight bristly legs

FANG-TASTIC!

All tarantulas have long fangs connected to large venom glands. The venom paralyses the prey and starts to digest it. Often, the tarantula ambushes prey from the entrance of its burrow and drags the prey inside to enjoy at its leisure.

DANCE PARTY

To attract a mate, the male **PEACOCK TARANTULA** will put on an impressive performance of leg-tapping, drumming and other nifty moves. The female will lay her eggs in a cocoon that she weaves herself, using silk made by her body. They also use silk to make 'trip wires' that alert them to the presence of prey.

TIGER BEETLES

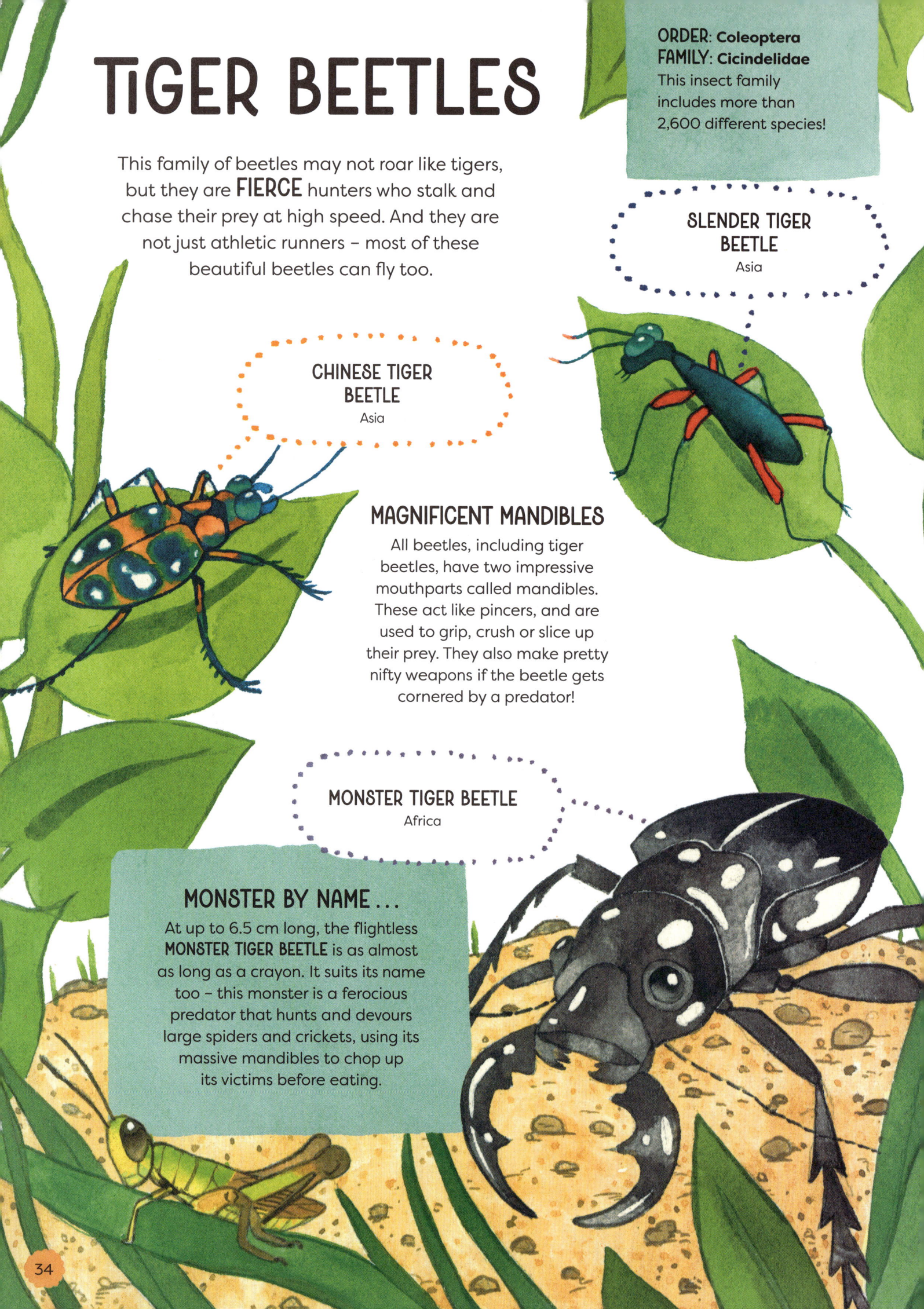

This family of beetles may not roar like tigers, but they are **FIERCE** hunters who stalk and chase their prey at high speed. And they are not just athletic runners – most of these beautiful beetles can fly too.

ORDER: Coleoptera
FAMILY: Cicindelidae
This insect family includes more than 2,600 different species!

SLENDER TIGER BEETLE
Asia

CHINESE TIGER BEETLE
Asia

MAGNIFICENT MANDIBLES

All beetles, including tiger beetles, have two impressive mouthparts called mandibles. These act like pincers, and are used to grip, crush or slice up their prey. They also make pretty nifty weapons if the beetle gets cornered by a predator!

MONSTER TIGER BEETLE
Africa

MONSTER BY NAME...

At up to 6.5 cm long, the flightless **MONSTER TIGER BEETLE** is as almost as long as a crayon. It suits its name too – this monster is a ferocious predator that hunts and devours large spiders and crickets, using its massive mandibles to chop up its victims before eating.

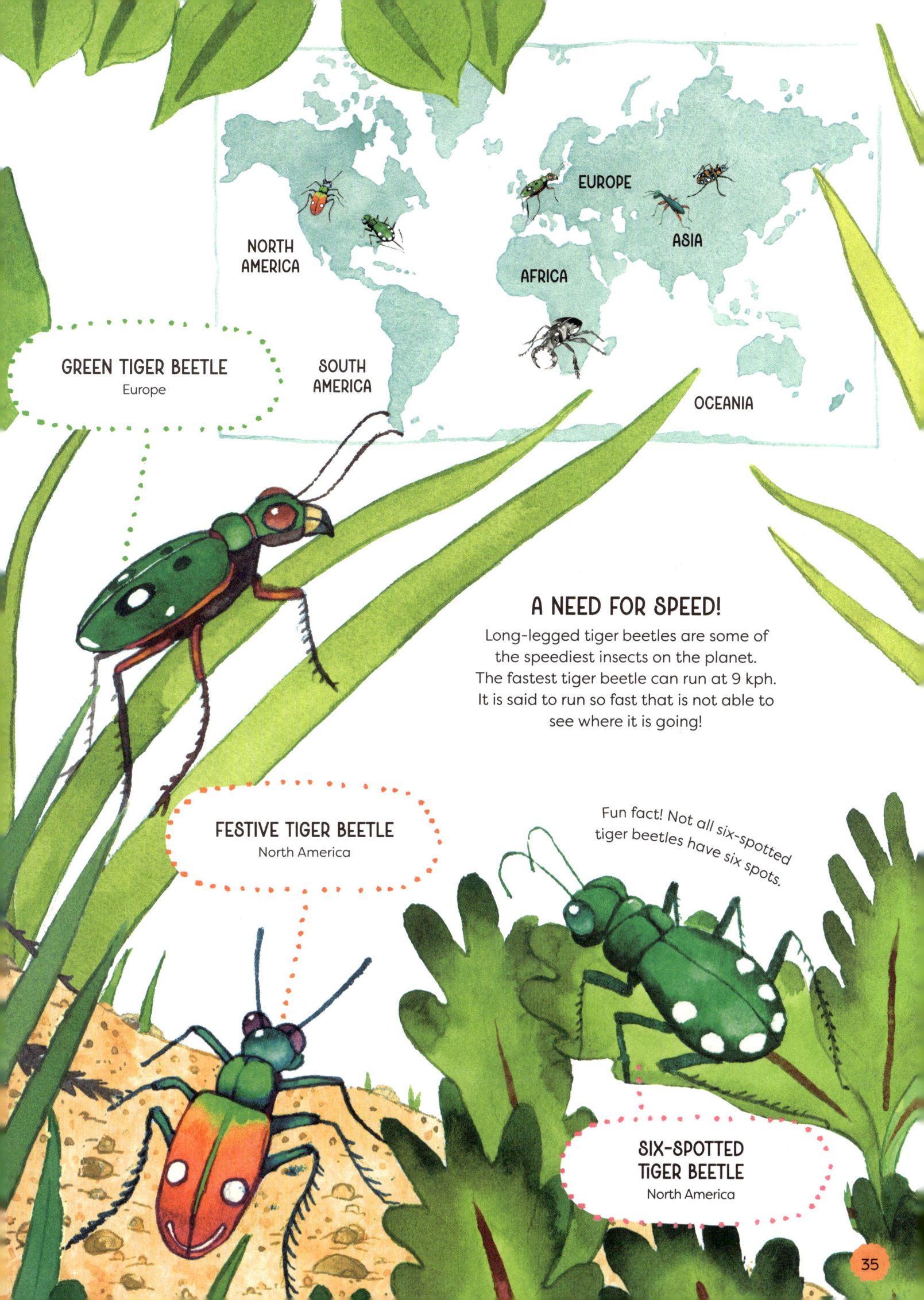

GREEN TIGER BEETLE
Europe

FESTIVE TIGER BEETLE
North America

A NEED FOR SPEED!
Long-legged tiger beetles are some of the speediest insects on the planet. The fastest tiger beetle can run at 9 kph. It is said to run so fast that is not able to see where it is going!

Fun fact! Not all six-spotted tiger beetles have six spots.

SIX-SPOTTED TIGER BEETLE
North America

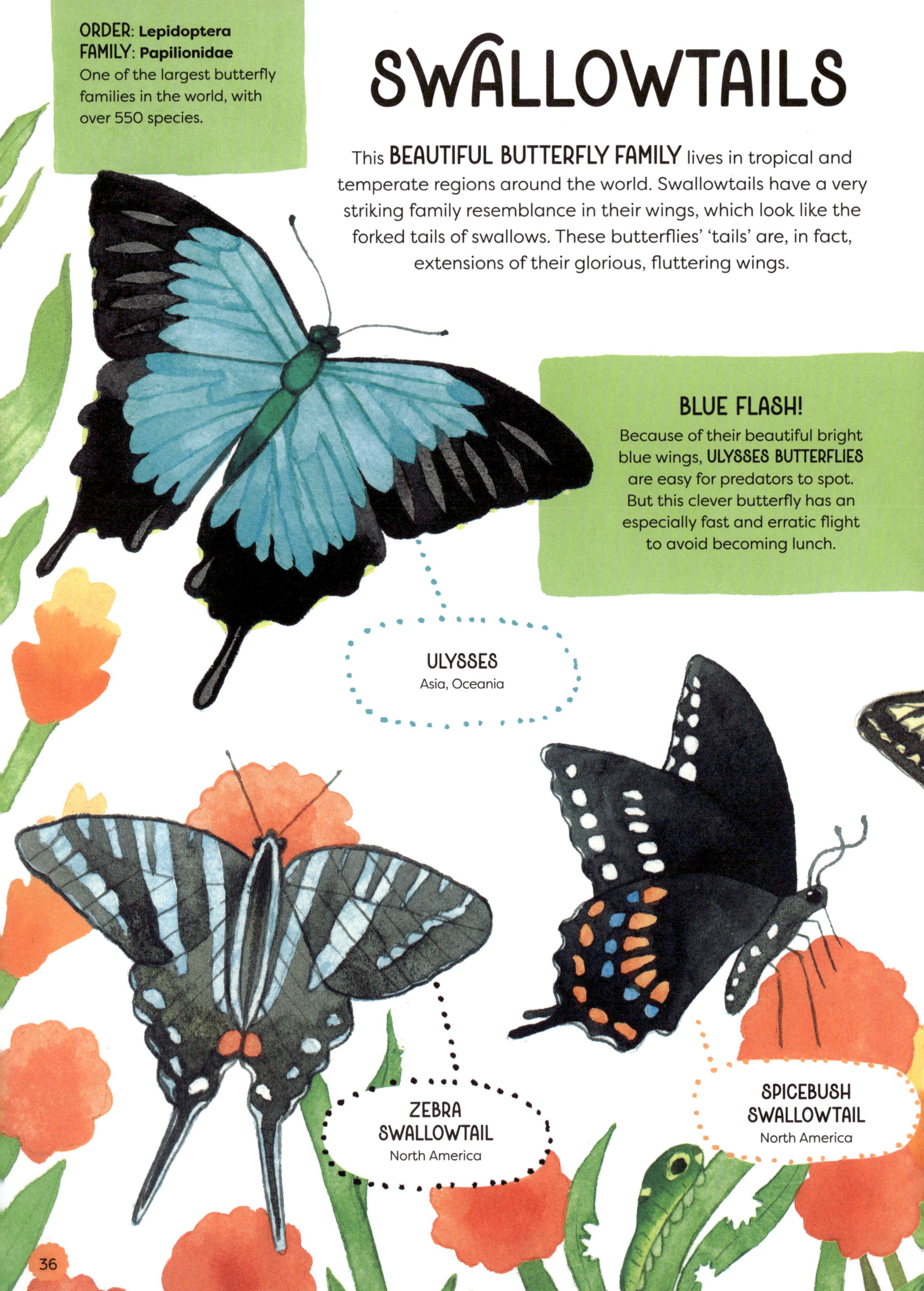

ORDER: Lepidoptera
FAMILY: Papilionidae
One of the largest butterfly families in the world, with over 550 species.

SWALLOWTAILS

This **BEAUTIFUL BUTTERFLY FAMILY** lives in tropical and temperate regions around the world. Swallowtails have a very striking family resemblance in their wings, which look like the forked tails of swallows. These butterflies' 'tails' are, in fact, extensions of their glorious, fluttering wings.

BLUE FLASH!
Because of their beautiful bright blue wings, **ULYSSES BUTTERFLIES** are easy for predators to spot. But this clever butterfly has an especially fast and erratic flight to avoid becoming lunch.

ULYSSES
Asia, Oceania

ZEBRA SWALLOWTAIL
North America

SPICEBUSH SWALLOWTAIL
North America

COMMON ROSE
South and Southeast Asia

NORTH AMERICA

SOUTH AMERICA

EUROPE

AFRICA

ASIA

OCEANIA

Like many butterflies, the common rose has brightly coloured spots on its wings to warn predators that it tastes bad.

OLD WORLD SWALLOWTAIL
Europe, Asia, North America

ASIAN SWALLOWTAIL
Asia

HEADS OR TAILS?

A swallowtail has a very clever way of defending itself. When it closes its wings, its 'tails' look like antennae and the eyespots like eyes. If a predator grabs this end of the butterfly, thinking it is the head, the butterfly has more chance of escaping with its life!

37

HAWKMOTHS

ORDER: Lepidoptera
FAMILY: Sphingidae
There are a whopping 1,450 members in this family!

If the Moth Awards existed, hawkmoths would win first prize for '**MOST SKILLED FLIERS**'. Not only are they fast, but they are also able to hover in place. Sometimes called sphinx moths, members of this nectar-guzzling family can be found in a wide variety of habitats around the world.

WHITE-LINED SPHINX
Central and North America

Looks like a stout, fluffy bumblebee, but is a far superior flier.

NARROW-BORDERED BEE HAWKMOTH
Asia, Europe

OLEANDER HAWKMOTH
Africa, Asia, Hawaii

ELEPHANT HAWKMOTH
Central Europe

PROBING PROBOSCIS

The hawkmoth does not land on flowers to feed, as many insects do. Instead, it skilfully hovers in front of an open flower and uses its long straw-like organ called a proboscis to slurp up the delicious nectar. Handily, it can curl up the proboscis when it's finished.

38

HUMMINGBIRD HAWKMOTH
Europe, Eurasia

LIME HAWKMOTH
Asia, Europe

IS IT A BIRD . . . OR A MOTH?
When the daytime-flying **HUMMINGBIRD HAWKMOTH** hovers to drink from a flower, it beats its wings so fast they make a humming sound. This is why it is sometimes confused with the hummingbird birds found in the Americas.

This skull-marked moth squeaks when it is alarmed by expelling air out of its proboscis.

AFRICAN DEATH'S HEAD HAWKMOTH
Southern Europe, Africa

NORTH AMERICA

SOUTH AMERICA

EUROPE

AFRICA

ASIA

OCEANIA

JUMPING SPIDERS

ORDER: Araneae
FAMILY: Salticidae
There are approximately 6,600 species of these acrobatic arachnids. These little spiders are not dangerous to humans.

Do you come from a big family? Jumping spiders sure do. These arachnids form the biggest spider family in the world, and they are **ADAPTABLE** little beasts. Jumping spiders can live pretty much anywhere, from humid rainforests to the driest of deserts – and the walls of your house. But best of all, they can jump!

YOUR BIGGEST FAN

Like many other spiders, the **FLYING PEACOCK** puts on a show to attract a mate that involves drumming, tapping and the enthusiastic waving of legs. However, this little show-off has an extra trick up its hairy sleeve – a colourful, fanlike flap on its body that it can wave around like a flag.

FLYING PEACOCK SPIDER
Australia

REGAL JUMPER
North America

BEARDFOOTED SPIDER
Europe, North Africa

Has one set of extra large legs!

40

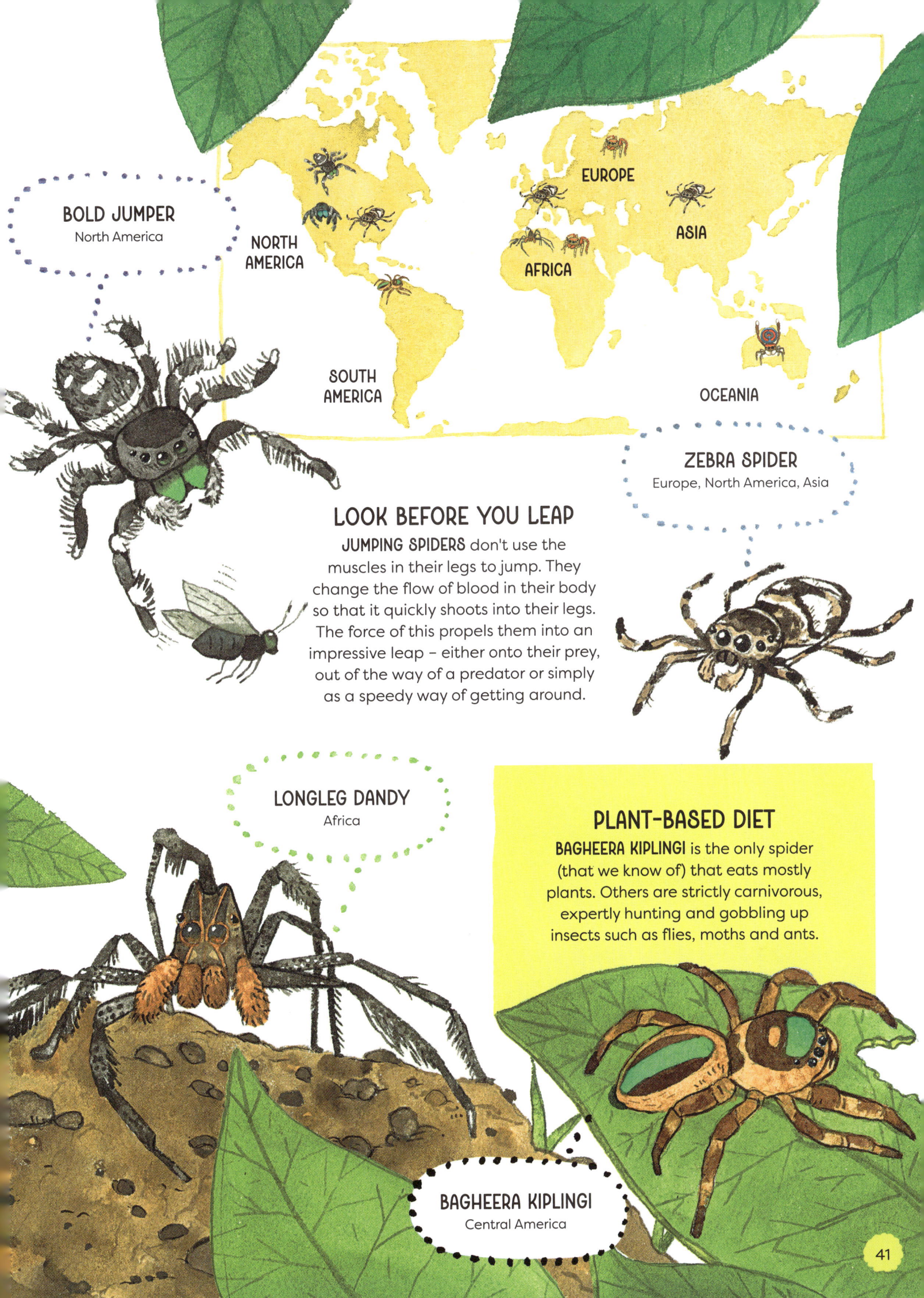

BOLD JUMPER
North America

ZEBRA SPIDER
Europe, North America, Asia

LOOK BEFORE YOU LEAP
JUMPING SPIDERS don't use the muscles in their legs to jump. They change the flow of blood in their body so that it quickly shoots into their legs. The force of this propels them into an impressive leap – either onto their prey, out of the way of a predator or simply as a speedy way of getting around.

LONGLEG DANDY
Africa

PLANT-BASED DIET
BAGHEERA KIPLINGI is the only spider (that we know of) that eats mostly plants. Others are strictly carnivorous, expertly hunting and gobbling up insects such as flies, moths and ants.

BAGHEERA KIPLINGI
Central America

COBRAS

This fork-tongued family can be found slithering around in southern Africa and South Asia. Known for their venom-filled **FANGS** and menacing hoods, cobras are fearsome animals, but it helps to know that baby snakes are called 'snakelets'. Aw.

ORDER: Squamata
FAMILY: Elapidae
This family also includes mambas, kraits, sea snakes and coral snakes.

KING COBRA
Asia

WHO NEEDS TO CHEW?

Snakes feed mostly on rodents and lizards, but cobras will also eat other snakes! They swallow their meals whole – burp! – and can go months, or even years, without eating.

The forest-dwelling king cobra is the world's longest venomous snake – it can grow up to 3.5 m long.

BACK OFF!

Many cobras, including the **MONOCLED COBRA**, will raise a hood around its head if threatened. At the same time, it raises its body off the ground and lets out a warning hiss. The cobra's hood is an extension of its ribs and muscles that it can expand to make itself look bigger and more intimidating.

MONOCLED COBRA
Asia

SAMAR COBRA
Southeast Asia

RED SPITTING COBRA
Africa

Red spitting cobras can spit venom into their victim's face from as far as 2.5 m away! Thankfully, it's not deadly to humans.

EGYPTIAN COBRA
Africa

INDIAN COBRA
India

INDIAN COBRA

Most snakes are shy and avoid human company, preferring to live in rural habitats. The **INDIAN COBRA**, however, can also be found hanging out in villages and cities across India, where there is a plentiful supply of rats for them to eat.

CHAMELEONS

Most species of chameleon live in Africa, but a few can be found on other continents. All travel on four legs, have eyes that can swivel around independently of each other (perfect for giving side-eye) and **LONG, STICKY TONGUES**. Many chameleons also have another trick up their sleeves – they can change colour!

ORDER: Squamata
FAMILY: Chamaeleonidae
There are more than 200 different species of chameleon in the family.

PARSON'S CHAMELEON
Madagascar

A SLIP OF THE TONGUE?

The **PARSON'S CHAMELEON** shoots out its long tongue at great speed to catch insects to eat. At the tip of its tongue is a sticky substance that allows the hungry chameleon to pick up the insect and pull it back into its mouth. All chameleons have these talented tongues, which can be up to three times longer than their bodies.

INDIAN CHAMELEON
Sri Lanka, India, Pakistan

JACKSON'S CHAMELEON
East Africa

Miniature Triceratops or species of chameleon? You decide!

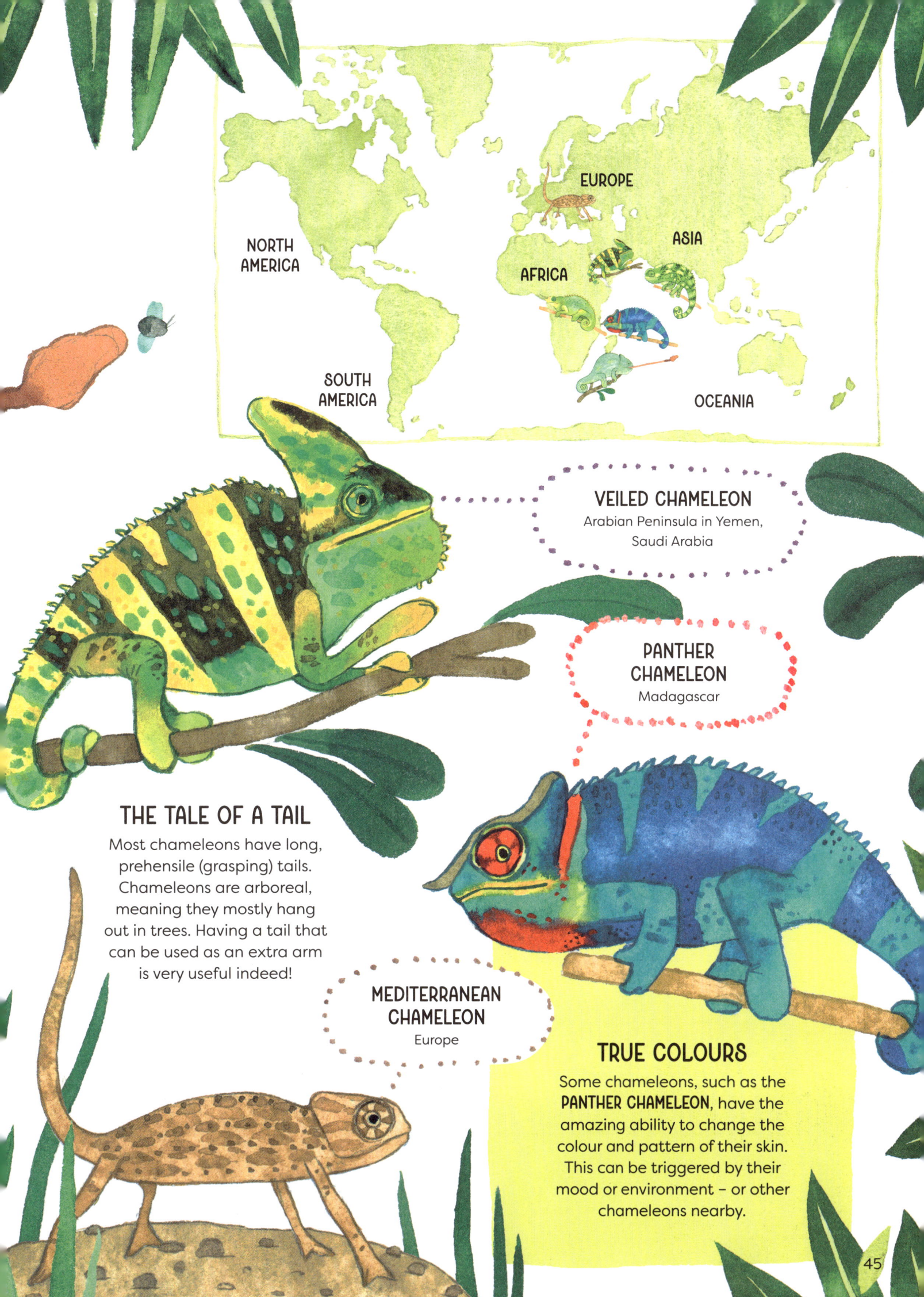

NORTH AMERICA
SOUTH AMERICA
EUROPE
ASIA
AFRICA
OCEANIA

VEILED CHAMELEON
Arabian Peninsula in Yemen, Saudi Arabia

PANTHER CHAMELEON
Madagascar

MEDITERRANEAN CHAMELEON
Europe

THE TALE OF A TAIL

Most chameleons have long, prehensile (grasping) tails. Chameleons are arboreal, meaning they mostly hang out in trees. Having a tail that can be used as an extra arm is very useful indeed!

TRUE COLOURS

Some chameleons, such as the **PANTHER CHAMELEON**, have the amazing ability to change the colour and pattern of their skin. This can be triggered by their mood or environment – or other chameleons nearby.

THE OCELLATE RIVER STINGRAY...

Get ready for two fascinating **UNDERWATER** animals. These graceful rays may come from different families, but they are related by order (Myliobatiformes) and have a lot in common, despite living in very different types of watery world.

The **OCELLATE RIVER STINGRAY** prefers a less salty environment than its bluespotted cousin and can be found in several South American rivers. In the rainy season the forest floors around the rivers can flood, and stingrays can be seen swimming around the trees. Just like its Asian cousin, the ocellate river stingray has a venomous sting.

Eyespot pattern on skin to confuse predators

Large, circular body shape

A SANDY BED

It can get very hot in the summer months in South America, but this is not a problem for the ocellate river stingray. It buries itself in the cool, sandy riverbed during the day, which also keeps it out of sight of anything that may want to eat it!

YUM!

The ocellate river stingray eats fish and crabs but will also feast on the larvae (the young) of water-dwelling insects.

VERSUS THE BLUESPOTTED RIBBONTAIL RAY

The **BLUESPOTTED RIBBONTAIL RAY** glides through the warm tropical oceans of Asia. It has a venom-tipped tail, but this shy creature would rather swim away from trouble than use its lethal weapon. The bright blue spots on its skin are there to send a message to its enemies – back off!

Tail patterned with two blue stripes

Large, protruding eyes

BABY RAYS
Ribbontail eggs are hatched inside their mum's body. They are born as teeny tiny live rays soon after!

SEAFOOD PLATTER
Rays dine on sand-worms, shrimps, crabs and small fish. With eyes on top of its body, it can see above itself as it lies on the ocean floor, waiting for a tasty snack to swim by.

STING-LESS RAYS
Manta rays are a type of stingray that have lost their not-so-secret weapon (their stinger) over time. They are also HUGE – the largest of the species has a wingspan of around 7 m!

GLOSSARY

ANTENNAE (singular: antenna) The two feelers attached to the head of insects, used for touching and smelling.

ARACHNID An animal that belongs to the class Arachnida. This includes spiders such as tarantulas.

BILL Another word for a bird's beak.

BURROW An underground hole or tunnel dug by an animal for shelter.

HABITAT The natural home of an animal or a plant; for example, a forest or a desert.

INSECTIVORES Animals that mainly eat insects.

MAMMAL A warm-blooded animal that has a backbone, produces milk for its young, has fur or hair on its body and has a skeleton. Humans, foxes and raccoons are all mammals.

MARSUPIAL A mammal that carries its young in a pouch on the front of its body. Koalas are marsupials.

NECTAR A liquid rich in sugar made by the flowers of plants. Bees use nectar to make honey.

NOCTURNAL Describes animals that are more active at night. Foxes and owls are mostly nocturnal.

OMNIVOROUS Describes creatures that eat both plants and animals.

PREDATOR An animal that hunts and eats other animals.

SEMI-AQUATIC Describes a living thing that spends some of its time in water.

TALONS The large, hooked claws of a bird, mostly birds of prey.

TEMPERATE Describes an environment that is neither very hot nor very cold.

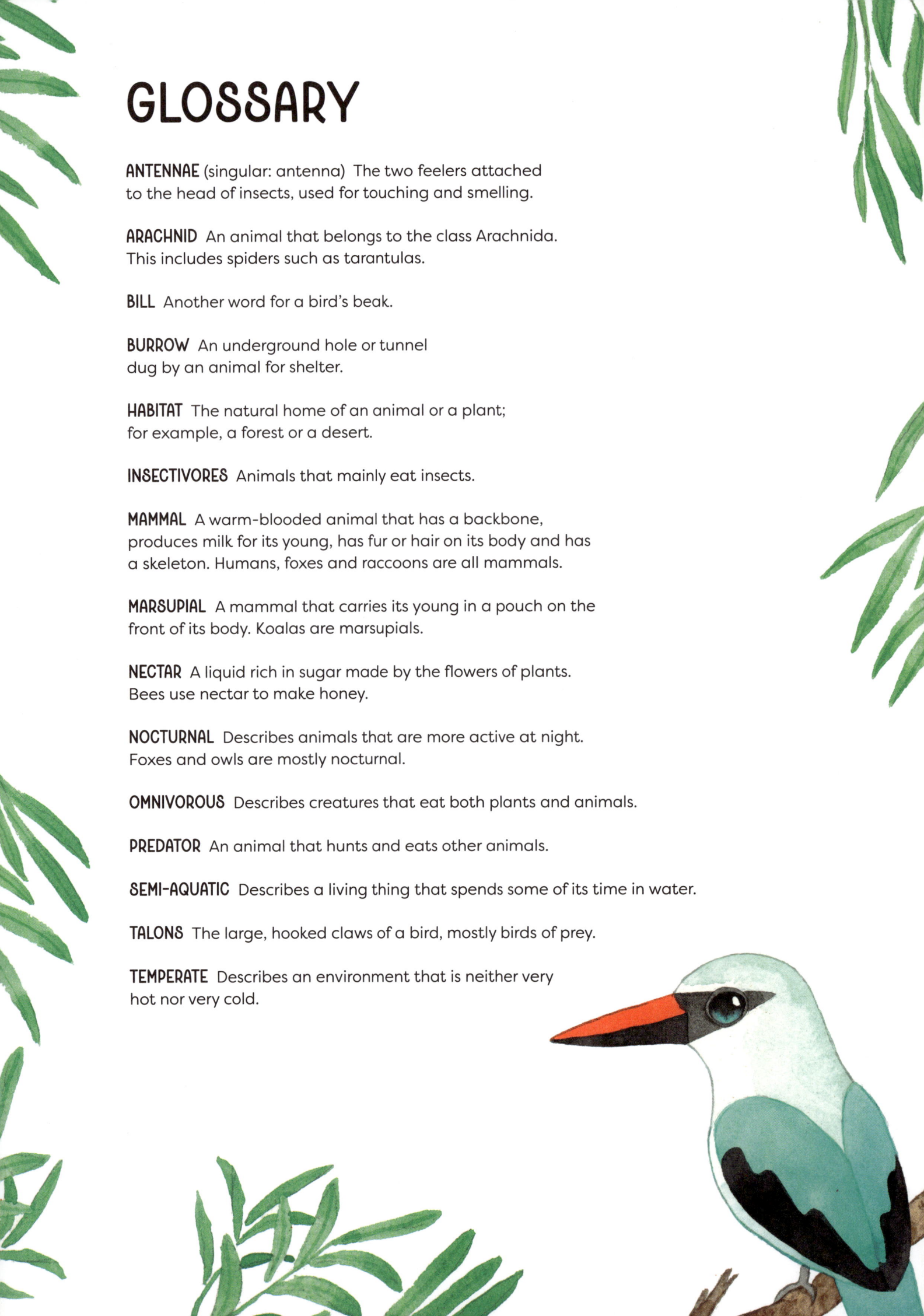